Over 50 Tasty Mariju[ana]

Baked

By Yzabetta Sativa

GREEN CANDY PRESS

BAKED: Over 50 Tasty Marijuana Treats
Published by Green Candy Press
San Francisco, CA

Copyright © 2011 Yzabetta Sativa

ISBN 978-1-931160-80-3

Photographs © Brody Bruce
Additional Photos © Stoned Rosie

This book contains information about illegal substances, specifically the plant Cannabis and its derivative products. Green Candy Press would like to emphasize that Cannabis is a controlled substance in North America and throughout much of the world. As such, the use and cultivation of cannabis can carry heavy penalties that may threaten an individual's liberty and livelihood.

The aim of the Publisher is to educate and entertain. Whatever the Publisher's view on the validity of current legislation, we do not in any way condone the use of prohibited substances.

Printed in China by Oceanic Graphic Printing

Sometimes Massively Distributed by P.G.W.

Contents

Introduction

I tried to quit smoking for over ten years to no avail. Every time I quit smoking cigarettes it would be smoking a joint that would bring me back to the habit. The most delicious thing, my favorite cigarette of all, was the one I would smoke after I had smoked a joint. As time passed I developed asthma and found during heat waves it was impossible to breathe. I felt horribly guilty for smoking and mentally raked myself over the coals for every cigarette I smoked. I figured it was only a short amount of time before I was going to go insane and take all those around me along for the ride.

One day I was being harassed by an avid non-smoker about when I was going to quit and I decided to disclose my vice so as to explain why I had been failing at quitting for over a decade. Well, he looked me straight in the face and in a laissez-faire tone of voice asked "Why don't you eat your pot instead of smoking it?" A light bulb went on and the sky opened up and for the first time I thought it just might be possible for me to quit smoking.

I did some research and found out that THC isn't water soluble. I studied the history of the use of pot, especially its Indian past. I experimented with different kinds of cannabis and eventually got Baked Butter down to an art form. I quit smoking and commenced with the eating of my pot. I was astonished to find that I now prefer the high I get from eating it. Whenever I smoked it there was this moment, right before the baked feeling set in, where my heart would palpitate and I'd feel like I'd had too much coffee and for a few moments would have to confront my own mortality. I'm happy to see that part of the intoxication vanish.

Another up side to eating my pot instead of smoking it is that my $140 a week habit is now a $140 a month habit. Combine the reduction of that cost with the money I saved by quitting smoking I managed to save, in a year and a half, a down payment for a house. I bought the house, moved my trusty crock pot along with all my other worldly possessions and, quite frankly, never looked back. I quickly got sick of pot brownies and started developing other yummy concoctions which I have put together in this cookbook.

How to Make Baked Butter

Place powdered pot and butter or margarine in a regular crock pot. A mini crock pot (1½-quart) is best. Regular size crock pots are only good if you're cooking three or four pounds of butter or margarine at a time.

Heat butter or margarine and powdered pot together in the crock pot on low for at least 12 hours but ultimately for 24 hours, covered. Strain the cooled butter or margarine through a strainer, lined with a layer of cheesecloth into the large bowl. Twist pulp in the double layer of cheese-cloth to get out all the liquid butter or margarine you can. Refrigerate to quicken cooling. When cool cut into large pieces, and place Baked Butter or margarine in sandwich bags for freezing in ½ cup quantities.

I personally don't strain the butter or margarine when it's done, if not out of abject laziness then for the added fiber in my diet. The only thing you have to be careful of, if you choose not to strain, is that a ½ cup of butter or margarine with the powdered pot in it does not actually measure a ½ cup of butter or margarine. I measure ½ a cup plus a dollop, if you will, to even out the score.

It used to be that people would use "shake" or low grade pot for making Baked Butter or margarine. However, more recent studies show that the superiority, potency and staying power of the pot are greatly improved

INGREDIENTS

1 lb. of butter or margarine (margarine just doesn't work the same but if you're lactose intolerant then by all means use margarine or canola oil)

½ ounce of good pot ground to a powder (grind the pot up by using a coffee grinder, pepper grinder or blender—though when I do it in a blender I add the butter or margarine pre-melted to the blender.)

To begin, you will need the pot and the butter.

Grind the pot to a fine powder using a coffee grinder.

Place ingredients into a small crock pot on low heat.

Allow ingredients to melt together, then simmer for over 24 hours.

Over a bowl, pour the ingredients into a strainer.

Squeeze the liquid through, and let the Baked Butter cool.

with good pot as opposed to "shake." In Canada we're able to purchase some wonderful, hydroponically grown pot which has been my personal preference since Ted Marchildon invented that hydroponic Ferris wheel of his.

This Baked Butter will keep a long time in the freezer and you can use it just as you would use any butter or margarine in any recipe, be it a savory or sweet recipe. You can enjoy it in smaller amounts spread on your toast, on your pancakes, or drizzled over popcorn. Each person only needs about 2 teaspoons of butter or margarine to get baked.

N.B. You can substitute the butter with margarine, vegan margarine, or canola oil. I don't advise using any other oil as it will compromise the taste and deliciousness of the recipes.

A Wee Bit about Weed

I do most, if not all of my baking, with what is affectionately called BC Bud. Thing is, it is actually grown locally and hydroponically and doesn't come from British Columbia. BC Bud has been parented by a British Columbian clone that sometimes is referred to as White Widow because of how caked the flowers are. This particular strain of weed is a 60% indica, 40% sativa hybrid that is lusciously heady and altogether charming.

Here in Canada there's a lot of smack talk about pot (seeing as how it's our second largest agricultural crop), so it's hard to believe anything about the infamous "White Widow." My botanically dense, plant-killer mentality thinks that it's really one sub strain or another of Northern Lights – but don't quote me on that.

Indica buds are compact, weighty, short and fat. The thing with indicas is that they smell "skunky" and their smoke is so thick that a small toke can induce coughing. The best indicas have a tranquil sort of "social high" which makes one chill and take in the scenery rather than pseudo-philosophically analyze the scenery to dullard death.

Sativa, on the other hand, has long, medium-thick buds that smell more tangy than sweet; if indica smells "skunky", then sativa smells like dirt or mud. The smoke is smooth and gives a kind of frenetic and confusing high. In short; sativa gets you high and indica gets you stoned. That's pretty much the extent of my scientific knowledge of weed botany.

The most anyone really know goes as follows: most of the THC, the medicinal ingredient, is in the flower buds of the female cannabis plant, with some in the leaves too. When I make Baked Butter I use the flower buds of really good pot. One could use the leaves or the stalk as well as what is known as "shake", but you wouldn't get as potent a butter which may be your intended goal. It's a personal choice.

The Disclaimer
Marijuana is illegal whether you smoke it or bake with it
if you don't have a prescription for it

Do not eat and drive.

Know your tolerance, whether you are new to smoking pot or have been using copious amount for years. The first time you try eating pot you should eat just a small amount and wait for an hour and a half. At that point you will be feeling the effects of the THC; take note of how you feel and the next time you ingest, adjust the dosage. Always eat the amount recommended in each of the recipes. Eating marijuana gives the same effects as smoking it, but often last two or three times longer, which you should keep in mind at all times.

Don't eat pot on an empty stomach. Sure, some people will tell you it's better on an empty stomach but, in my opinion, it's best to have something to eat beforehand. Having something in your stomach seems to help prevent you from eating too much or getting hit too hard. To quote Martha Stewart, "it's a good thing."

You must be patient; don't just keep eating your freshly baked pot dessert until you feel the effects. I can't say this enough: it will take a while for it to hit you. Make very sure when you get the munchies you don't eat more then, either. Absorption though the stomach is slower than through the lungs, so it can take well over an hour and a half for you to feel "high". THC gets absorbed at a different rate every time you eat it. The effects of eating cannabis can last several hours, while they tend to wear off within an hour when smoked. If you fall asleep or pass out, know that your digestion will slow down which means you could wake up still high.

Make no mistake, you can eat far too much and the results of that are unpleasant, to say the least. If you overindulge, it can last a long time, possibly as long as 10 hours. This is not as fun as it sounds; if you're in the wrong place or with the wrong people it can become very upsetting. Pot is meant to be fun and relaxing, and dizziness, sweating, nausea, vomiting, possible crying, and freaking out is definitely not fun.

If you do eat too much there are a couple of things you can do. Stay low to the ground, to avoid unpleasant head rushes, and try taking a high dose of vitamin C (200mg or more) to help to make you feel better. You can also trying eating something relatively heavy, meaning not a salad but a slice of pizza. The best antidote is to crawl in bed and go to sleep.

You, as the consumer, have responsibility in three areas: your own situation, health, and safety. The situational responsibilities include the avoidance of risky situations, not using when you're alone, nor using it because someone persuasive talked you into it. Health responsibilities include not eating too much or mixing it with other drugs, attentiveness to all the possible health consequences of drug use, and not using a drug recreationally during periods of excessive stress in order to self medicate. If you are self medicating, in my opinion you have a problem that eating pot isn't going to help. Safety-related responsibilities include using the smallest dose necessary to achieve the desired effects, using only in laid back surroundings with supportive friends and not doing anything ridiculous like operating heavy machinery.

I am highlighting responsible drug use as a chief prevention technique in my personal harm-reduction drug policy, and because I care. We all want to enjoy pot, so just don't be stupid and have fun!

Bars & Squares

Marshmallow Squares

Dreamy, light and fluffy, these will melt in your mouth

Preheat oven to 325° F.

In a bowl, thoroughly combine the Baked Butter or margarine, flour and sugar to form a soft dough.

Pat the dough into an 8 x 8-inch glass baking dish.

Bake for 8 to 10 minutes, then remove from oven.

Cut the marshmallows in half, then place them on top of the base until it is completely covered.

Increase the heat in the oven to 375° F.

Return the marshmallow-covered base to the oven for 5 minutes or until all the marshmallows have melted together. Allow to cool.

Cover the whole top with the cream cheese frosting. Serve. One square should get you Baked

INGREDIENTS

½ cup of Baked Butter

2 tablespoons of brown sugar

1 cup of flour

½ bag of marshmallows

1 453g tub of cream cheese frosting

French Canadian Sugar Squares

A maple syrupy homage to French Canadian sugar pie

Grease a 9 x 9-inch square pan. Preheat oven to 350° F.

Cut the ½ cup of Baked Butter into the 1 cup of flour with the 2 tablespoons of sugar. Press the mixture into the square pan. Bake this crust for 15 minutes.

Combine the cream, egg, and tablespoon of flour, with the 2 tablespoons of butter, maple syrup, and brown sugar. Pour this mixture onto the shell and return the pan into the oven.

Bake for another 25 to 30 minutes or until the mixture swells. Cool thoroughly before cutting into 20 squares. One or two squares should get you baked.

INGREDIENTS

½ cup of Baked Butter

1 cup of all-purpose flour

2 tablespoons of sugar

¼ cup of heavy cream (or soya cream/coconut milk)

1 egg

1 tablespoon of flour

2 tablespoons of Baked Butter

1 cup of maple syrup

1 cup of brown sugar

Scottish Brownies

The shortbread crust makes these brownies
mind-meltingly delicious

Preheat oven to 300° F.

In a medium bowl, stir together 1 cup of rice flour and the sugar. Cut in the Baked Butter or margarine until the mixture is crumbly. Press the mixture firmly into the bottom of a 9 x 9-inch baking pan.

Bake for 20 to 25 minutes in the preheated oven until firm and only ever-so-slightly golden. Set aside to cool.

Preheat oven to 350° F.

In a medium sized mixing bowl, mix together ¼ cup of the flour, baking powder, and cocoa powder. Make a well in the center of these ingredients, and add the egg, vanilla, and sweetened condensed milk. Mix this batter until it is well combined. Stir in the chocolate chips and the pecans if you choose to use them. Spread the mixture over the cooled crust.

Bake for 20 minutes in the preheated oven, until brownies begin to pull away from the edges and the top appears dry.

Cool thoroughly and cut into squares. Store tightly covered at room temperature. One brownie should get you baked.

INGREDIENTS

1 cup of rice flour
¼ cup of white sugar
½ cup of softened Baked Butter
¼ cup of all-purpose flour
¼ cup of unsweetened cocoa
  powder
½ teaspoon of baking powder
1 egg
1½ teaspoons of vanilla extract
1 (14-ounce) can of sweetened
  condensed milk
1 cup of chocolate chips
¾ cup of chopped pecans (optional)

New Old Fashioned Squares

A fresh twist on a classic

Preheat oven to 350° F. Grease a 12 by 12-inch square pan.

Cream the Baked Butter or margarine with an electric hand mixer until fluffy. At high speed add in the sugar and eggs and beat well for about 2 minutes.

With a spoon stir in the melted chocolate, flour, nuts, and salt until the batter is an even color.

Pour the batter into the prepared baking pan. Bake for 20 to 25 minutes. Cool thoroughly before cutting into 24 squares. One square should get you baked.

INGREDIENTS

½ cup of Baked Butter

1¾ cups of brown sugar

2 eggs

¾ cup of melted chocolate

1 cup of almonds

1 cup of cashews

1 cup of pecans

1½ cups of flour

½ teaspoon of salt

Captain Morgan Blondies

Enough rum to make even the most fierce pirate smile

Preheat oven to 350° F. Grease a 9 x 9-inch baking dish; glass works the best.

Sift together the flour, spices, sugar, and salt; set them aside.

In a large mixing bowl, beat together the Baked Butter or margarine and eggs until creamy. Beat in the milk as well as the rum.

Gradually stir the flour mixture into the egg mixture. Stir in the chips and nuts after that.

Pour the batter into the prepared baking dish. Bake for 30 minutes or until the blondies start to begin to pull away from the edges and the top appears dry.

Cool thoroughly and cut into squares. Store tightly covered at room temperature. One blondie should get you baked.

INGREDIENTS

1 ½ cups of all-purpose flour

1 teaspoon of ground cinnamon

1 teaspoon of ground ginger

½ teaspoon of ground nutmeg

¼ teaspoon of ground allspice

¾ cup of sugar

pinch of salt

⅔ cup of Baked Butter

3 large eggs

¼ cup of milk

3 tablespoons of rum

⅔ cup of butterscotch chips

½ cup of chopped nuts (use your favorite)

Crack

So addictive, you won't
want to eat just one

These bars are affectionately called "Crack" because on more than one occasion I found myself eating more than the desired amount because they taste so good. I've become addicted to them. Be extra careful with any of the desserts you find yourself addicted to.

Mix the entire list of ingredients thoroughly together in a bowl.

Pour into 9 x 9-inch baking dish; glass works the best.

Bake at 375° F for about 8 to 10 minutes or until it looks golden-brown and bubbly. When it's done take it out of the oven and pull the "crack" away from all four sides.

Allow to cool for 5 minutes, and then mark in squares with a sharp knife. Loosen the edges again and allow them to cool thoroughly before removing the squares from the pan.

One square will get you baked.

INGREDIENTS

2 cups of instant oats

1 cup of packed brown sugar

½ cup of melted Baked Butter

½ teaspoon of pure vanilla extract

Dreamy Raspberry Bars
Three layers of dreamy buttery, jammy, vanilla goodness

Preheat oven to 375° F.

Combine the first 7 ingredients (butter, flour, soda, sugars, milk and egg yolks) together. Press into a 9 by 9-inch pan. Bake for 12 minutes until the edges are lightly golden brown.

When you remove the base from the oven spread the raspberry jam evenly across it. Set the pan aside.

Change oven temperature to 350° F.

Beat the egg whites with an electric hand mixer until they form stiff peaks. Fold the other ingredients (sugar, butter, vanilla, and nuts) gently into the egg whites until combined. Pour over the raspberry jam covering the base.

Bake for 20 to 25 minutes or until golden brown. Allow to cool thoroughly before cutting. Cut into 12 squares. One square is enough to get you baked.

INGREDIENTS

½ cup of Baked Butter

1 ½ cups of flour

1 teaspoon of soda

¼ cup of brown sugar

¼ cup of white sugar

1 tablespoon of milk

1 egg

½ cup of really good raspberry jam

2 tablespoons of butter

1 cup of white sugar

2 separated eggs

¼ teaspoon of salt

1 teaspoon of vanilla

1 cup of chopped pecans

Cookies

Chocolate Chip Cookies

Not like grandma used to make

Preheat oven to 300° F.

Cream the Baked Butter or margarine with both of the sugars using an electric mixer on medium speed until fluffy (approximately 30 seconds).

Beat in the egg and the vanilla extract for another 30 seconds.

In a mixing bowl or on wax paper, sift together the dry ingredients three times and beat into the butter mixture at low speed for about 15 seconds.

Stir in the chocolate chips.

Using an ice cream scoop or a serving spoon, drop cookie dough (about 2 tablespoons of dough works best) onto a greased cookie sheet about 2½ inches apart. Gently press down on the dough to spread out the cookie into a 2-inch circle.

Bake for about 18 minutes or until nicely browned around the edges. Bake the cookies a little longer for crunchier cookies. Two cookies should do the trick.

INGREDIENTS

½ cup of softened Baked Butter

1 cup of light brown sugar

3 tablespoons of granulated sugar

1 large egg

2 teaspoons of vanilla extract

1¾ cups of all purpose flour

½ teaspoon of baking powder

½ teaspoon of baking soda

½ teaspoon of salt

1½ cups of semi-sweet chocolate chips

Spice Cookies

These cookies contain the finest spices and
are drizzled with vanilla glaze

Preheat oven to 350° F. Grease a cookie sheet.

In a mixing bowl cream the Baked Butter and sugar together with a hand mixer on medium. Beat in the egg. Stir the molasses into the bowl of batter.

On to a piece of wax paper sift all the dry ingredients together including the spices. Sift three times.

Combine the pre-sifted dry ingredients into the bowl, alternating with coffee. Drop the batter from a spoon onto cookie sheet about 2 inches apart. Bake for 8 to 10 minutes.

When the cookies are done allow them to cool.

While they're cooling make a glaze with the combination of powdered sugar, vanilla, and tablespoons of milk. Drizzle the glaze over the cookies. Two cookies should do the trick.

INGREDIENTS

COOKIES

½ cup of Baked Butter

½ cup of brown sugar

1 egg

⅓ cup of molasses

2¼ cups of flour

2 teaspoons of ground, dried
   coriander

2 teaspoons of baking soda

3 teaspoons of ground, dry ginger

1 teaspoon of cinnamon

½ teaspoon of cloves

¼ teaspoon of salt

⅓ cup of really strong coffee

GLAZE

2 cups of powdered sugar

1 teaspoon of vanilla extract

3 tablespoons of milk

Double Chocolate Delights

Indulge the chocolate lover in your life

with these delicious treats

Cream the Baked Butter or margarine with an electric hand mixer in a medium sized bowl. Add the melted chocolate, then the sugar, and then the eggs. Beat until thoroughly combined. Set this mixture aside.

In another bowl or on waxed paper combine the flour, cocoa, baking powder, and salt. Sift these ingredients together three times.

Fold the dry ingredients into the butter mixture alternately with the chocolate milk. Add the vanilla extract. Cover the bowl with plastic wrap and refrigerate for 3 hours.

Preheat oven to 400° F.

Roll the dough into a log shape then slice about ¼ of an inch thick. Place slices, 1½ inches apart, on an ungreased, large cookie sheet. Bake for 10 minutes.

Remove from oven and let cool. Two cookies should be enough to get you baked.

INGREDIENTS

½ cup of Baked Butter

1 cup of sugar

¼ cup of melted chocolate

1 egg

⅓ cup of chocolate milk (or chocolate soya milk)

1 teaspoon of vanilla extract

2 cups of flour

1 tablespoon of cocoa

1½ teaspoons of baking powder

Pinch of salt

Fresh Fragrant Fancies
A favorite best enjoyed with a steaming cup of mint tea

In a medium bowl, cream together the Baked Butter, white sugar, and icing sugar until the mixture is light and fluffy. Mix in the lavender, mint, and lemon zest.

Combine the flour, cornstarch, and salt; mix these dry ingredients into the batter until well blended.

Divide the dough into two balls, wrap them separately in plastic wrap and flatten to about 1 inch thickness. Refrigerate the dough until firm, for approximately one hour.

Preheat oven to 325° F.

On a lightly floured surface, roll the dough out to ¼ inch thickness. Cut into shapes with cookie cutters. Cookie stamps will work well on these too if you're feeling extra creative and so inclined. Place the cookies on cookie sheets.

Bake for 18 to 20 minutes in the preheated oven, just until the cookies begin to brown at the edges. Cool for a few minutes on the baking sheets then transfer to wire racks to cool the cookies completely. Two to three cookies should get you baked.

INGREDIENTS

¾ cup of oil

½ cup of softened Baked Butter

⅔ cup of white sugar

¼ cup of sifted icing sugar

2 tablespoons of finely chopped, fresh lavender

2 teaspoons of chopped, fresh mint leaves

1 teaspoon of grated lemon zest

2½ cups of all-purpose flour

½ cup of cornstarch

Pinch of salt

Peanut Butter Cup Cookies

So good they ought to come with a warning label

Preheat oven to 375° F.

Sift together the flour, salt, and baking soda on a piece of waxed paper or in a bowl and set aside.

Cream together the Baked Butter or margarine, sugar, peanut butter, and brown sugar until fluffy. Beat in the egg, vanilla, and cream and blend the mixture together until it's all combined. Add the flour mixture a bit at a time; mix it thoroughly.

Shape the dough into 24 balls and place each ball into the cup of an un-greased mini muffin pan.

Bake at 375° for about 8 to 10 minutes. Remove them from oven and immediately press a mini peanut butter cup into each ball. Do this as fast as you can.

Cool the cups before you carefully remove them from the baking pan. I use a butter knife to kind of lift the cup out much like I would a mini muffin. One cup should do the trick. If it doesn't then split a cup in half, eat one half and then wait at least 30 minutes before eating the other half.

INGREDIENTS

- ¾ cup of packed brown sugar
- ¼ cup of white sugar
- ½ cup of peanut butter
- ½ cup of softened Baked Butter
- 1 lightly beaten egg
- 2 tablespoons of 10% cream (or soy cream)
- 1 teaspoon of pure vanilla extract
- 1¾ cups of all-purpose flour
- 1 teaspoon of baking soda
- ½ teaspoon of salt
- 24 miniature peanut butter cups

White Queen Cookies

White chocolate and lavender make this
a recipe fit for royalty

Preheat oven to 350° F.

In a medium bowl, blend the Baked Butter or margarine, sugar, and lavender until smooth. Then add the egg, milk, and vanilla.

In another bowl, mix the oatmeal, flour, and baking powder together; add in the chocolate chips.

Mix both of your blends together until they form a soft dough.

Place spoon sized drops of the cookie dough onto a very lightly greased or non-stick cookie sheet and bake for about 8 to 10 minutes or until soft but firm, if that makes sense

Allow the cookies to cool. Two cookies should do the trick.

If you want to change things up a bit you can also add chopped, blanched almonds or shredded coconut; about one half of a cup should do.

INGREDIENTS

½ cup of Baked Butter

½ cup of brown sugar

1½ tablespoons of culinary grade
lavender flowers

1 egg

2¼ tablespoons of milk

1 teaspoon of vanilla extract

1 cup of oatmeal

1½ cups of flour

¾ teaspoon of baking powder

1 cup of white chocolate chips

Mint Chocolate Bundles

Cookies topped with a healthy measure of mint chocolate

In a large pan over low heat, melt the Baked Butter or margarine, and blend in the sugar and water. Add the chocolate chips and stir until partially melted.

Remove the pan from the heat and continue to stir until the chocolate is completely melted. Pour into a large bowl and let stand to cool for 10 minutes.

With a hand mixer at high speed, beat the eggs into the chocolate mixture, one at a time. Reduce the speed of the mixer to low and add the dry ingredients, beating until blended.

Cover the dough in plastic wrap and let chill in the fridge for about an hour and a half.

Preheat oven to 350° F.

Roll dough into balls and place on an ungreased cookie sheet about 2 inches apart. Gently smack the top of each ball to create a flat surface. Bake for 8 to 10 minutes.

Remove from oven and immediately place chocolate covered mints on top of each cookie. Let cool for 5 minutes, or until the mints are melted, then spread each mint over the whole cookie. Two cookies should get you baked.

INGREDIENTS

¾ cup of packed brown sugar

¾ cup of white sugar

¾ cup of Baked Butter

2 tablespoons of carbonated water
   (I use Perrier)

2 eggs

2½ cups of all-purpose flour

1¼ teaspoons of baking soda

½ teaspoon of salt

2 cups of chocolate chips

40 chocolate covered mints

Lemon Verbena

In a pinch, substitute grated lemon rind or
even lemon grass for lemon verbena

In a mixing bowl, cream the softened Baked Butter or margarine with the
sugar then add the egg and blend well. Set the bowl aside.

On a piece of wax paper, sift together the flour, cream of tartar, and salt.
Sift three times.

Stir the sifted ingredients into the creamed fusion until well mixed. Then,
add the chopped verbena. Cover the bowl with plastic wrap or a well-fit-
ted lid. Chill overnight.

When you are ready to bake, preheat oven to 350° F. Lightly grease a
cookie sheet.

Roll chilled dough into 1-inch balls and pat the tops down carefully and
lightly. Bake for 8 to 10 minutes. Allow the cookies to cool. Two cookies
should get you baked.

INGREDIENTS

½ cup of softened Baked Butter

¾ cup of sugar

1 egg

1¼ cups of flour

½ teaspoon of cream of tartar

3 tablespoons of finely chopped fresh
   lemon verbena (1 tablespoon if
   dried)

Pinch of salt

Peanut Butter Cookies

Smooth or crunchy — the choice is yours

Preheat oven to 325° F. Lightly grease a cookie sheet.

Cream the Baked Butter or margarine, peanut butter, and both of the sugars together. Blend the egg into the sugar mixture and set aside.

In a separate bowl or on wax paper combine the flour, soda and salt. Sift together three times.

Stir the dry ingredients into the sugar mixture and blend thoroughly. Roll the mixture into 1-inch balls. Place the balls about an inch apart on a cookie sheet and press the tines of a fork into each ball to flatten.

Bake for 12 to 15 minutes. Cool. Two cookies should get you baked.

INGREDIENTS

½ cup of peanut butter

½ cup of Baked Butter

½ cup of white sugar

½ cup of brown sugar

1 egg

1½ cups of flour

1 teaspoon of baking soda

Pinch of salt

Lavender Love Bites

More like a tender kiss than a bite

Preheat oven to 350° F. Grease a cookie sheet.

Cream together the Baked Butter or margarine and sugar. Beat the egg, and blend it into the butter and sugar. Mix in the lavender flowers and the flour. Drop the dough by teaspoonfuls onto a cookie sheet.

Bake 15 to 20 minutes, or until golden. Remove the cookies to cooling racks so that the underside of the cookie doesn't get soggy. One to two cookies should get you baked.

INGREDIENTS

½ cup of Baked Butter

½ cup of sugar

1 egg

2 teaspoons of lavender flowers

1½ cups of all-purpose flour

Cakes

Aloha Hawaiian Bread

Aloha has many meanings; in this case delectable

Preheat oven to 350°. Line a well greased loaf pan on the bottom with waxed paper.

In small bowl thoroughly smash bananas and set aside.

Mix the sugar, shortening, and Baked Butter or margarine in another mixing bowl and blend thoroughly. Add the smashed bananas and eggs, and mix this all together.

On a piece of waxed paper or in a bowl, combine the flour, baking powder, and salt. Sift these ingredients together three times through.

Add the dry ingredients into the wet and stir until the flour is moistened. Pour into the prepared loaf pan. Drop loaf pan gently onto the countertop three or four times to remove any air bubbles.

Bake for 1 hour at 350°. Be sure to test for doneness by sticking a toothpick or wooden skewer into the center of the loaf; don't take the loaf out of the oven until the skewer comes out dry. When cooled thoroughly cut into 12 slices. One slice should do the trick.

INGREDIENTS

¾ cup of coarsely chopped
   macadamia nuts
½ cup of dark brown sugar
½ cup of Baked Butter
½ cup of shortening
¾ cup of brown sugar
¼ cup of white sugar
1 egg
1 cup of smashed banana
1¼ cups of pastry flour
½ teaspoon of baking powder
Pinch of salt

Banana Cream Cake

The more ripe the banana, the more intense the flavor

Grease and flour a 9-inch spring form pan. Preheat oven to 350° F.

With a hand mixer, beat the Baked Butter or margarine and sugar together until it's very fluffy and then beat it for about 2 minutes longer. Add each egg, one at a time, and beat the mixture back to the fluffy consistency after each egg.

Beat the already smashed bananas into the mixture. Add the liqueur and mix thoroughly. Set liquid mixture aside.

In another bowl or on a sheet of waxed paper combine the flour, baking powder, baking soda, and salt. Sift the dry ingredients together three times. Once sifted, add the dry ingredients to the wet ingredients a third at a time to make sure it's all blended.

Pour the batter into the pan. Gently drop the pan onto a counter or flat surface about three times to remove the air bubbles.

Bake for 40 minutes. Be sure to test for doneness. When cooled thoroughly, ice the cake if you have a sweet tooth (recipe follows). If you don't, feel free not to bother with the icing. Cut into 12 slices. One slice should get you baked.

INGREDIENTS

½ cup of Baked Butter

2 eggs

1 cup of smashed bananas

⅔ cup of sugar

¼ cup of Irish Cream liqueur

2 cups plus 2 tablespoons of flour

1 teaspoon of baking powder

1 teaspoon of baking soda

A pinch of salt

INGREDIENTS

½ cup of Baked Butter

3 cups of icing sugar

¼ cup of Irish Cream liqueur

⅓ cup of melted chocolate chips

BANANA CREAM ICING

With an electric hand mixer cream the Baked Butter or margarine until fluffy.

Blend in the melted chocolate and icing sugar alternately with the Irish Cream.

Beat on high until your desired consistency is achieved—normal icing consistency. If it's too dry add more Irish Cream. If it's too wet add more icing sugar.

Ice the Banana Cream Cake and serve. Be extra careful, though, as it has the double whammy of Baked Butter in the cake as well as the icing.

The Devil's Manna

A devilishly good chocolate cake — ice it any way you like

Preheat oven to 350° F. Prepare the pans by greasing and flouring two 8-inch cake pans.

Combine the cocoa, baking soda, and salt together in a bowl or on waxed paper. Sift together three times and set aside.

In a medium bowl, cream the Baked Butter or margarine and sugar together with an electric hand mixer until fluffy. Add the eggs one at a time until well blended. Add the melted chocolate until the color of the batter is consistent.

Fold in the dry ingredients alternately with the buttermilk; incorporate the dry and wet in thirds. Take your time as it's important to get all the ingredients incorporated well.

Pour the batter evenly into both pans. Gently drop the pans onto a counter or flat surface to remove the air bubbles. Drop the pans on the counter three times each.

Bake for 35 to 40 minutes. Make sure to test for doneness. Cool and ice with any kind of icing you like (maybe even Banana Icing). Cut into 12 slices. One slice should get you baked.

INGREDIENTS

½ cup of Baked Butter

2 eggs

½ cup of melted chocolate

1 cup of buttermilk (or vegan
    substitute, follows)

2 cups of cake flour

1 teaspoon of baking soda

2 tablespoons of cocoa

¼ teaspoon of salt

VEGAN SUBSTITUTE
FOR 1 CUP OF BUTTERMIK:

¼ cup of silken tofu

½ cup plus 3 tablespoons of water

1 tablespoon of lemon juice or
    vinegar

Pinch of salt

Blend all ingredients together. Let
the solution stand for ten minutes
before adding to your recipe.

Sour Cream Cake
A deliciously playful mix of sweet and sour

Preheat oven to 350° F. Grease a 9 by 9-inch inch baking pan.

Combine the Baked Butter or margarine, brown sugar, and corn syrup. Spread mixture out evenly on the bottom of the prepared baking dish. Sprinkle the chopped nuts over the mixture in the pan.

Combine the remaining ingredients in a large mixing bowl. With an electric hand mixer beat the batter for 4 to 5 minutes at a medium speed until the batter is smooth. Pour the batter into the baking pan over the top of the nuts.

Bake for 50 minutes or until the cake passes the doneness test. Cool the cake in the pan for 2 minutes then loosen the edges from the side of the pan. Invert the cake onto a serving plate by putting the serving plate on top of the cake pan and flipping it. Allow the cake to cool for 5 more minutes. Cut into 20 pieces or more. One piece should get you baked.

INGREDIENTS

½ cup of Baked Butter

2 tablespoons of light corn syrup

½ cup of brown sugar

½ cup of chopped almonds

1 box of white or golden cake mix

2 eggs

1 cup of sour cream

¼ cup of water (I use Perrier)

Sensational Shortcakes

Light and fluffy — like walking on a cloud

Preheat oven to 400° F. Line a baking sheet with parchment paper.

Take the lemon rind and sugar and put them on a piece of waxed paper or a cutting board. With the back of a soup spoon, push the lemon rind into the sugar (like you would with garlic and salt) to create lemon sugar. Then, combine the lemon sugar with the flour, baking powder, salt, and dried oregano in a bowl. Mix these ingredients methodically.

Using a pastry cutter or two sharp knives, cut the cold Baked Butter or margarine into the dry ingredients, until the size of gravel (like you'd find in a fish tank, though that doesn't sound appetizing). Mix in the cream, incorporating the ingredients until just barely combined. It's very easy to over-mix this batter, which will make the cakes very dense and tough.

Roughly shape the shortcakes into hockey puck sized cakes and place them onto the prepared baking sheet. Bake the shortcakes for 15 minutes or until golden brown.

Remove from the oven and let cool. Garnish the shortcake with raspberries and whipped cream. One cake should do the trick.

INGREDIENTS

½ cup of cold Baked Butter

½ cup of half and half (10% cream)

2 tablespoons of freshly grated
    lemon rind

¼ cup of sugar

2 cups of flour

4 teaspoons of baking powder

½ teaspoon of salt

1 tablespoon of dried oregano

Raspberries and whipped cream for
    garnishing the shortcakes

Vienna Bundt Cake
Add kick with instant coffee or cappuccino

Preheat oven to 350° F. Generously grease and flour a 12-cup bundt cake pan.

Mix the Baked Butter or margarine, sugar, flour, cinnamon, instant coffee granules, and chopped nuts together until crumbly and set aside.

Combine the cake mix, water, oil, and eggs and beat with an electric hand mixer on low speed until it all comes together (that sounds dirty). Beat the mixture on a medium speed for another 4 minutes.

Pour ⅓ of the batter into the prepared bundt pan then sprinkle with ½ of the crumby mixture as evenly as possible. Repeat this step, using a second third of the batter and sprinkling the last half of the crumbly mixture. Top the whole thing off with the last third of batter.

Bake for 50 minutes or until the cake tests as properly done. Allow the cake to cool for 10 minutes then invert onto a serving plate. Cool completely.

If you like, you can sprinkle the top with icing sugar or mix 1 teaspoon of hot water into a cup of icing sugar and drizzle the glaze over the top of the bundt cake, allowing the glaze to dribble down the sides. Cut into 16 slices. One to one and a half slices should get you baked.

INGREDIENTS

½ cup of Baked Butter

½ cup of flour

1 cup of brown sugar

2 teaspoons of cinnamon

½ teaspoon of instant coffee (or instant cappuccino)

½ cup of chopped almonds

1 package of devil's food cake mix

1 cup of water

3 eggs

¼ cup of canola oil

Candies

Almond Toffee

This delectable buttery confection is easy to make

Generously grease a 10 by 10-inch baking pan.

Combine the sugar, salt, water, and Baked Butter or margarine in a large pan and bring the mixture to a rolling boil.

Add about a third of the almonds and cook, stirring constantly to prevent the toffee from scorching, until mixture reaches about 300° F (hard crack stage).

Use a candy thermometer to test temperature. Alternatively, use a clear drinking glass filled with cold water; drop a little of the molten syrup into the cold water and it will form hard, brittle threads when ready.

Remove the pan from the heat. Stir in the second third of almonds. Pour the candy into the well greased pan. Let the candy stand in a cool place until it hardens.

Remove the candy from pan, spread the melted chocolate over the top, and sprinkle with the last remaining third of almonds. When the choco-late is firm, break the candy apart by tapping it with a sharp knife across the surface. A small handful of candy, about the size of a brownie or a cookie, should be enough to do the trick.

INGREDIENTS

½ cup of Baked Butter

1 cup of chopped, blanched almonds

1 cup of sugar

½ teaspoon of salt

¼ cup of water

½ cup of melted milk chocolate chips

Chocolate Marsh-mellow Bites

These bites will gratify anyone with a sweet tooth

In a saucepan, combine Baked Butter, sugar, and vanilla with 10 ounces of the semi-sweet chocolate. Bring mixture to a slow boil and stir occasionally until it reaches the soft ball stage (238° F).

Use a candy thermometer to test temperature. Alternatively, use a clear drinking glass filled with cold water; drop a little of the candy into the cold water and it will form a soft, flexible ball when ready.

Remove the pot from heat, add the marshmallows and stir until thoroughly melted. Pour mixture onto a well-greased baking sheet and spread evenly.

Allow to cool to the touch then roll bite size pieces into round, smooth balls. Place back onto cookie sheet and allow to cool for one hour.

Melt the remaining semi-sweet chocolate in a saucepan, double boiler or using the microwave. Dip each ball in the melted chocolate and place back onto the cookie sheet. Allow to cool.

Melt white chocolate in a saucepan, double boiler or using the microwave. Drizzle the melted white chocolate over the bites in a decorative fashion.

Allow to cool. You'll make about 48 bites. 4 to 5 bites per should get you baked.

INGREDIENTS

2 cups of regular marshmallows

1½ teaspoons of vanilla extract

½ cup of Baked Butter

4 cups of cream (18%)

4 cups of sugar

1 pound of melted semi-sweet chocolate

4 ounces of melted white chocolate chips

Peanut Butter Bites

Chock full of nutty buttery goodness

Place the Baked Butter or margarine in a bowl and soften it with a wooden spoon. Blend in the corn syrup, peanut butter, salt, and vanilla, mixing it until creamy. Stir in the icing sugar.

Turn candy onto a pastry board and knead until it's blended and smooth. Gradually add the chopped nuts, pressing and kneading them into the dough.

With greased fingers, roll the fudge into 16 balls. Chill for at least 1 hour.

Serve chilled. One to one and a half pieces will do the trick.

INGREDIENTS

½ cup of Baked Butter

½ cup of light (or white) corn syrup

½ cup of peanut butter

½ teaspoon of salt

1 teaspoon of vanilla

3½ cups of sifted icing sugar (add more if the mixture is sticky)

¾ cup of chopped nuts (pecans or almonds or peanuts or a combination of all three; or omit, depending on your taste)

Baked Fudge

Exceptionally rich in either vanilla or chocolate flavors

Grease a 10 by 10-inch square pan.

Combine cocoa, sugar, and salt in a large saucepan. Add the milk gradually, mix thoroughly, and bring the mixture to a rapid or bubbly boil on high heat, stirring continuously.

Turn down to a medium heat and continue to boil the mixture without stirring until it reaches a temperature of 236° F, the soft-ball stage (when dropped into a bowl of very cold water it will form a soft ball which flattens on removal from the water).

Remove the mixture from heat. Add the Baked Butter or margarine and vanilla to mixture and then blend thoroughly until all the butter melts.

Allow the fudge to cool and then beat it like the Michael Jackson song. Cut it into 16 pieces. One to one and a half pieces will do the trick.

To make vanilla fudge, just leave out the cocoa.

INGREDIENTS

1½ cups of cocoa

6 cups of sugar

¼ teaspoon of salt

3 cups of milk

½ cup of Baked Butter

2 teaspoons of vanilla extract

Sesame Snaps

Tastes, crunches, and melts in your mouth just like brittle!

Spread sesame seeds on baking sheet and toast in a 350° F oven for 15 minutes or until golden.

Sprinkle half of the seeds over a greased 13 x 9-inch baking pan. Set aside.

In saucepan, bring the Baked Butter or margarine, brown sugar, and water to boil, stirring until internal temperature reaches 285° F – the soft crack stage. Use a candy thermometer to test temperature. Alternatively, use a clear drinking glass filled with cold water; drop a little of the candy into the cold water and it will separate into threads that are hard but not brittle.

Immediately remove the saucepan from the heat then stir in the baking soda as fast as possible.

Pour the syrup over the toasted sesame seeds in the prepared pan. Allow to cool for at least 5 minutes before sprinkling with reserved sesame seeds. Press lightly into toffee. Be careful though as hot candy can leave a bad burn.

Let cool until firm. Break the candy into pieces. The candy can be layered between waxed paper in an airtight container and stored for up to 1 month.

A handful of candy, about the size of a cookie, should get you baked.

INGREDIENTS

½ cup of Baked Butter

½ cup of sesame seeds

¾ cup of packed brown sugar

1 ½ tablespoons of water

⅓ teaspoon of baking soda

Butter Rum Fun

These squares are delicious and have a captivating aroma

Grease a 9 by 9-inch pan or large cookie sheet.

Mix the sugar, milk, and Baked Butter or margarine in a medium saucepan. Cook it over medium heat, stirring frequently, until the mixture begins to form a soft ball. Remove the saucepan from the heat.

Add the chocolate chips, marshmallow crème, rum flavoring, and nuts to the saucepan. Stir the mixture quickly until well combined.

Pour onto the prepared pan or large cookie sheet. Score the top immediately into 16 squares but don't cut the candy all the way through just yet.

Allow the candy to cool thoroughly then finish cutting thorough the squares. One square should get you baked.

INGREDIENTS

2 cups of sugar

¾ cup of evaporated milk

½ cup of Baked Butter

½ cup of semisweet chocolate chips

1 cup of marshmallow crème

½ teaspoon of rum flavoring

1 cup of chopped cashews

Cool Mint Patties

Mint smothered in decadent dark chocolate —
refreshing and euphoric

Use a mixing bowl to mix the corn syrup, peppermint extract, and slightly melted Baked Butter or margarine. Then add the sugar, a little bit at a time, and incorporate into the mix. Add the amount of food coloring to achieve your desired color and blend well.

Roll this mixture into small balls. Place them a couple of inches apart from each other on a cookie sheet that has been lined with wax paper. Use a fork to make each one flat.

Let the mint patties set in the refrigerator for several hours. Remove the patties from the refrigerator and let stand at room temperature for several days to dry out.

After a few days when the patties are dried out transfer them to a container with an airtight lid and store them in the refrigerator

You'll make about 24 patties. Eat 3 to 4 patties per (regular size) person to get baked.

INGREDIENTS

½ cup of light corn syrup

2 teaspoon of peppermint extract

½ cup of softened Baked Butter

2 drops of food coloring (optional)

9 cups of sifted powdered sugar
(about 2 pounds)

Orange Coconut Chews

A taste of the tropics in every bite

Preheat oven to 350° F. Grease a 9 by 9-inch pan.

In a saucepan, melt the Baked Butter or margarine then remove the saucepan from the heat.

Stir in the brown sugar, vanilla, and orange rind. Once those ingredients are well combined add the eggs.

In a bowl or on a piece of waxed paper combine the dry ingredients. Sift all the dry ingredients together three times. Combine the dry ingredients with the wet until completely mixed. Pour the batter into prepared baking dish.

Bake for 25 to 30 minutes. Cut into 16 squares when thoroughly cooled. If you like, roll each square into a ball and roll in more coconut. One to one and a half pieces/squares/balls will get you baked.

INGREDIENTS

½ cup of Baked Butter

2 cups of brown sugar

2 slightly beaten eggs

2 teaspoons of vanilla

3 teaspoons of freshly grated
    orange rind

1 cup of flour

1 teaspoon of salt

2 teaspoons of baking powder

2 cups of shredded coconut

2 cups of chopped dates

Chocolate Chews

Chewy scrumptiousness for any chocolate lover

Preheat oven to 325° F. Grease a 8 by 8-inch pan.

In a bowl or on a piece of waxed paper sift all the dry ingredients together except the quick oats. Sift 3 times. Set aside.

In a mixing bowl combine all the wet ingredients then beat well—well over 200 strokes by hand or about 2 minutes with an electric hand mixer. With a spoon, stir in the oatmeal and the nuts. Spread the mixture evenly into the pan.

Bake for 30 minutes. Allow the candy to cool thoroughly then cut into 12 squares. Roll each square into a ball and roll in sugar to coat each ball. One piece/square/ball will get you baked.

INGREDIENTS

½ cup of Baked Butter

½ cup of melted chocolate

½ teaspoon of vanilla

¾ cup of quick oats

¼ cup of your favourite chopped nuts

¾ cup plus 2 tablespoons of sifted flour

1 teaspoon of salt

¾ cup of sugar

1 egg

Gluten-Free

Vanilla Crisps

Vanilla lovers will find these cookies irresistible

Beat together the Baked Butter or margarine, sugar, and the salt until fluffy. To this mixture add the egg, vanilla, and milk. Slowly stir so as to incorporate the flour and baking powder, until totally combined. Wrap the bowl in plastic wrap.

Chill the dough until cold.

Preheat oven to 350° F.

Scoop the dough into a piping bag. If you don't have a piping bag, you can use a freezer bag with a small corner cut out. Evenly squeeze quarter-sized dollops of dough out onto a cookie sheet lined with parchment paper. Try to space the cookies out by half an inch.

Bake the cookies for approximately 10 to 14 minutes, or until edges are lightly browned. Allow the cookies to cool thoroughly before storing them. One to two cookies should get you baked.

INGREDIENTS

½ cup of softened Baked Butter

1 cup of granulated sugar

1 egg

1 tablespoon of vanilla extract

1 tablespoon of milk

1 teaspoon of gluten-free baking powder

1½ cups of all purpose gluten-free flour

A pinch of salt

Oatmeal Raisin Cookies

Soft and chewy old-fashioned goodness

Preheat oven to 350° F.

Cream the sugars and the Baked Butter or margarine together, with an electric hand mixer, until fluffy. To this mixture add the eggs, one at a time, until everything is carefully integrated into the batter. Once that is done, add in the vanilla.

In a separate bowl, or on a piece of wax paper, sift all dry ingredients (except the oats); sift together three times.

Methodically combine the dry ingredients into the creamed butter and sugar until well blended. Next, stir in the oats and raisins. Cover the bowl with plastic wrap and chill it for at least 2 hours.

When done chilling roll the dough into balls and place at least 2 inches apart on a parchment-lined cookie sheet. Bake for 8 to 10 minutes, or until lightly brown.

Let them cool on a wire rack before eating. Two cookies should do the trick.

INGREDIENTS

½ cup of Baked Butter

½ cup of granulated sugar

½ cup of firmly packed brown sugar

1 egg

½ teaspoon of gluten-free vanilla extract

1 cup of gluten-free all purpose flour

½ teaspoon of baking soda

1 teaspoonof baking powder

¼ teaspoon of salt

2 teaspoons of cinnamon

1½ cups of gluten-free oats

½ cup of raisins

Sweet Shortbread

Just four ingredients make this recipe short and sweet

Preheat oven to 300° F.

You will need to use a sifter for the dry ingredients. Sift everything but the Baked Butter or margarine, three times through. Clean and dry your hands, then mix the Baked Butter or margarine into the flour mixture and knead the dough.

Once the dough is soft, like mashed potatoes, knead it for another five minutes. Put the dough, covered, into the refrigerator and let it set for about an hour or so.

Take dough out of the refrigerator and roll shortbread into small ball like shapes, then press them lightly to make them flat. Place onto a lightly greased baking pan and bake in the oven for 20 to 25 minutes, until the edges are ever so slightly browned.

Make sure you let the cookies cool at least 10 minutes to let them set and harden before removing them. This will make about 24 cookies but you'll only need 1 to 2 cookies to get baked.

INGREDIENTS

½ cup of cornstarch

½ cup of icing confectioners' sugar

1 cup of rice flour

¾ cup of Baked Butter

Cranberry Bread

Delicious for breakfast, an afternoon snack, or dessert

Preheat oven to 350° F. Grease and flour an 8 x 8-inch loaf pan (glass is best).

In a medium bowl, whisk together the gluten-free flour, salt, baking powder (gluten-free), and xanthan gum, using a wire whisk.

Using a mixer set on medium high, cream the Baked Butter or margarine and sugar until fluffy. Add the egg yolks and beat on medium high until combined.

Next, add the orange rind and then a little of the flour. Mix. Add orange juice. Mix. Repeat this process until all the flour and juice are mixed. Stir in the cranberries using a wooden spoon.

Beat the egg whites until stiff and then fold them gently into the batter.

Pour the batter into a loaf pan and place in center of oven. Bake for about 50 minutes, 60 if needed. The loaf should be golden in color.

When cool, cut the loaf into 12 slices. One slice should do the trick. For an extra zing spread Baked Baked Butter or margarine on the slice before eating.

INGREDIENTS

2 cups of gluten-free flour mix

1 teaspoon of salt

5 teaspoons of baking powder

2 teaspoons of xanthan gum

½ cup of Baked Butter

½ cup of sugar

3 eggs, separated

½ tablespoon of grated orange rind

¾ cup of orange juice (fresh squeezed is best)

1 cup of fresh cranberries, cut in half

Ginger Snap Cookies

Ginger adds a hot kick to these finely spiced treats

Preheat oven to 350° F.

Cream the first 4 ingredients together.

Add the rest of the ingredients and mix well.

Form into 1½ inch mud pies (like when you were a kid) and cover in sugar.

Place on pan with parchment paper approximately 2 inches apart.

Bake for 8 minutes at 350° F (it can depend on pans and ovens, but this works for me). Let the cookies cool. One or two cookies should do the trick.

INGREDIENTS

¾ cup of softened Baked Butter

1 cup of sugar

2 eggs

⅓ cup of blackstrap molasses

2¼ cups of buckwheat flour

¼ teaspoon of salt

2 teaspoons of baking soda

1½ tablespoons of cinnamon

1½ tablespoons of ground ginger

1½ teaspoons of allspice

Canadian Maple Cookies

This gluten-free take on a Canadian treat can be made with or without nuts

In a mixing bowl, blend all ingredients thoroughly. Cover the bowl with plastic wrap.

Chill the dough overnight.

Preheat oven to 350° F. Lightly grease a cookie sheet.

Roll the dough into 1-inch balls and arrange on the cookie sheet. Using the spoon or the bottom of a glass, press each ball of dough out to about a quarter inch thickness. Bake for 10 to 12 minutes.

Once cooled, two cookies should do the trick.

INGREDIENTS

½ cup of Baked Butter

2 cups of brown rice flour

½ cup of maple syrup

1 teaspoon of salt

2 teaspoons of vanilla extract

2 slightly beaten eggs

2 cups of ground nuts, almonds work really well

Sugar-Free

Chocolate Cookies

A sugar-free treat that will satisfy your chocolate craving

Cream together the Baked Butter or margarine together with the sugar substitution. Add the eggs, vanilla, and milk and mix thoroughly.

Add half of the flour, mixing well, and then stir in the melted chocolate. Add the rest of the flour and mix well.

Roll the dough into small balls. Put flour on your hands to keep the dough from sticking to you. Press down with your fingers on the top of each cookie.

Bake cookies for 18 to 20 minutes. Allow to cool. One to two cookies should get you baked.

INGREDIENTS

¼ cup of sugar substitute like Equal

½ cup of Baked Butter

2 eggs

1 teaspoon of pure vanilla extract

¼ cup of milk

2½ cups of cake flour

2 ounces (2 squares) of melted
   unsweetened chocolate

Strawberry Cookies

A taste of summer that will leave you tickled pink

Preheat oven to 350° F.

Cream the Baked Butter or margarine and gelatin in a bowl.

In another bowl, mix the baking powder, flour, egg, and vanilla extract together.

Add this mixture to the cream of butter and gelatin; beat with an electric mixer for about 2 minutes.

Roll out the dough and cut into square shapes. Place the cut cookies on a non-greased cookie sheet.

Bake cookies in the oven for about 10 to 12 minutes. Let them cool. One to two cookies should do the trick.

INGREDIENTS

½ cup of Baked Butter

1½ cups of flour

½ teaspoon of baking powder

1 package of strawberry gelatin

1 teaspoon of vanilla extract

1 egg

Sweet Enough Peanut Butter Cookies

A traditional favorite that never fails to please

Preheat oven to 400° F. Grease a cookie sheet.

Mix the Baked Butter or margarine, peanut butter, vanilla extract, maple syrup, and egg together thoroughly. Then, add flour and baking powder to the liquid mixture. Beat the mixture well.

Make small balls, smaller than a golf ball, out of the dough. Place them on the prepared baking sheet. Flatten them with the help of a fork.

Bake the cookies for about 8 to 10 minutes. Make sure that the cookies are not over-baked.

Two cookies should do the trick.

INGREDIENTS

1 cup of flour

½ cup of Baked Butter

½ cup of natural peanut butter

⅓ cup of sugar-free maple syrup

½ teaspoon of baking powder

1 teaspoon of vanilla extract

1 egg

Oatmeal Cookies

Natural oatmeal goodness baked into every bite

Preheat oven to 350° F. Lightly grease a cookie sheet.

Combine all the ingredients in a large bowl. Mix well.

Roll the dough into small balls. Place them on the prepared cookie sheet. Then, press down with a fork.

Bake for about 10 to 12 minutes or until the cookies turn golden brown. Two cookies should do the trick.

INGREDIENTS

½ cup of Baked Butter

1 cup of flour

1 cup of oatmeal

1 cup of unsweetened applesauce

½ cup of raisins

1½ teaspoons of cinnamon

¼ teaspoon of ground cloves

¼ teaspoon of ground nutmeg

1 teaspoon of baking powder

½ teaspoon of baking soda

1 teaspoon of vanilla extract

¼ cup of water

¼ cup of chopped pecans

2 eggs

Pinch of salt

Banana Cookies
As moist and tender as classic banana bread

Preheat oven to 350° F.

Combine bananas, oats, dates, Baked Butter or margarine, and vanilla and mix thoroughly. Allow the dough to rest for 20 minutes or so to let flavors blend.

Drop the dough by teaspoonfuls onto an ungreased cookie sheet and bake for 15 to 18 minutes or until golden brown.

Two cookies should get you baked.

3 bananas, smashed

2 cups of rolled oats

1 cup of chopped dates

½ cup of Baked Butter

1 teaspoon of vanilla extract

Maple Cookies

Taste the rich, golden, maple goodness in every bite

Preheat oven to 375° F.

Cream together the Baked Butter or margarine, maple syrup, vanilla, and egg. Add the flour and stir until well combined.

Drop the dough by spoon onto and ungreased baking sheet.

Bake for 10 to 12 minutes, until the bottoms of cookies are golden brown—but just the bottom, not the top. Two cookies should do the trick.

INGREDIENTS

½ cup of Baked Butter

½ cup of sugar-free maple syrup

1 egg

1 teaspoon of vanilla

1½ cups of flour

¼ teaspoon of salt

Spice Bars

Wonderfully moist and not too sweet —
an excellent treat for breakfast

Preheat oven to 350° F. Grease a 13 x 9-inch metal cake pan.

In large bowl, beat Baked Butter or margarine with granulated sugar substitute until fluffy. Beat the eggs into the mixture, one at a time.

Whisk together the flour, cinnamon, baking soda, salt, and nutmeg; stir the dry ingredients slowly into butter mixture alternately with applesauce. Do this at least two times so that you're making at least two additions of each.

Stir in the raisins and almonds. Scoop the batter into the prepared cake pan.

Bake the cake for about 40 minutes or until a toothpick can be inserted into the middle of the cake and come out clean. Let the cake cool; cut it into about 16 bars. One bar will get you baked.

INGREDIENTS

½ cup of softened Baked Butter

¾ cup of a granular sugar substitute like Splenda

1½ cups of unsweetened applesauce

3 eggs

2 cups of cake flour

2 teaspoons of cinnamon

½ teaspoon of ground nutmeg

½ teaspoon of allspice

1 teaspoon of baking soda

½ tsp of salt

1 cup of raisins

1 cup of slivered almonds

Vegan

Maple Oatmeal Chewies

A delectable combination of oatmeal, walnuts, coconut, and raisins, and more

Preheat oven to 350° F.

Cream Baked Vegan Margarine, sugar, brown sugar, maple syrup, baby food, corn starch, soy milk/almond milk, and vanilla in large bowl at medium speed with an electric mixer until well blended.

Combine the flour, baking soda, and salt. Mix into the creamed mixture. Stir in the oats, coconut, raisins, and walnuts.

Drop rounded teaspoonfuls of dough onto an ungreased baking sheet. Bake for 11 to 12 minutes for soft cookies, or 13 to 14 minutes for crispier cookies.

Remove the cookies to a cooling rack. This recipe should make about 3 dozen cookies. Two cookies should do the trick.

INGREDIENTS

½ cup of Baked Vegan Margarine
½ cup of brown sugar
½ cup of sugar
4 tablespoons of maple syrup
1 tablespoon of sweet potato baby food
1 teaspoon of corn starch
2 tablespoons of soy milk/almond milk
1 teaspoon of vanilla
1¼ cups of flour
½ teaspoon of baking soda
½ cup of quick oats
½ cup of shredded, unsweetened coconut
½ cup of raisins
½ cup of walnut pieces
Pinch of salt

Butterscotch Brownies

Looks like brownies; tastes like butterscotch pudding

Preheat oven to 350° F. Grease an 11 x 7-inch baking pan.

Melt the Baked Vegan Margarine in a large saucepan. Add sugar and beat the two together well until it's mixed. Cool the mixture slightly, and then beat in the baby food, corn starch, and vanilla.

Sift together the flour, salt, and baking powder. Stir it into the wet ingredients, and then add the nuts. Mix well.

Spread the brownies in the pan and bake for 30 to 35 minutes or until a light golden color.

Cool in the pan for 10 minutes, and then turn out. This is easiest if you up-end the pan over waxed paper, then turn the brownies right side up.

While the brownies are cooling, make the icing by creaming the margarine together with the icing sugar. Beat it until it's light, and then beat in the coffee mixture.

Spread the icing over the brownies. When the icing has set, cut the brownies into 24 squares. One square should do the trick.

INGREDIENTS

½ cup of melted Baked Vegan
   Margarine
1 cup of brown sugar
3 tablespoons of sweet potato baby
   food
1½ teaspoons of corn starch
1 teaspoon of vanilla
1 cup of flour
¾ teaspoon of baking powder
½ cup of chopped pecans
Pinch of salt

ICING

½ cup of vegan margarine
3 cups of sifted icing sugar
2 teaspoons of instant coffee,
   dissolved in 2 tablespoons of hot
   water

Regular Special Brownies

The original "baked" dessert; an all-time favorite

Preheat oven to 350° F. Grease an 8 by 8-inch pan.

In a medium bowl, combine the melted Baked Vegan Margarine and cocoa powder and beat until cocoa is completely dissolved. Blend in the sugar.

Add the egg replacer to the mixture until it is evenly dispersed throughout the mix. While beating (with an electric hand mixer, of course), add the soy milk and vanilla extract a little at a time until it's all evenly mixed.

Sift together the flour, salt, and baking powder in a small bowl. Sift it three times, mostly for good measure.

Stir the dry ingredients into the chocolate mixture with a spoon, just until no more flour is visible. Do not over-mix! Fold in the chocolate chips.

Spread the mixture in the pan and bake for 25 to 28 minutes. Cool completely before cutting. Cut into 16 squares. One brownie should get you baked.

INGREDIENTS

½ cup of melted Baked Vegan Margarine

½ cup of unsweetened cocoa

1 cup of sugar

Egg replacer for 2 eggs

3 tablespoons of soy milk

2 teaspoons of vanilla extract

½ cup of flour

¼ teaspoon of salt

¼ teaspoon of baking powder

¾ cup of vegan chocolate chips

Mockolate Chip Cookies

A delicious vegan twist on a cookie classic

Preheat oven to 350° F.

Sift together the flour, salt, and baking soda in a bowl and set aside.

In a separate large bowl, beat together the Baked Vegan Margarine, sugar, brown sugar, vanilla, and egg replacer.

Add the dry ingredients to the wet ingredients (that's why they're in a large bowl) and stir until the dough is combined well. Stir in the vegan chocolate chips.

Drop one-inch spoonfuls of dough onto an ungreased cookie sheet. Bake for 8 to 10 minutes, until edges are golden brown. Two cookies should get you baked.

INGREDIENTS

1½ cups of flour

½ teaspoon of salt

½ teaspoon of baking soda

½ cup of Baked Vegan Margarine

½ cup of brown sugar

½ cup of sugar

½ teaspoon of vanilla extract

Egg replacer for 1 egg

½ cup of vegan chocolate chips

California Gold Bars

Jam-packed with the flavor of apricot

Preheat oven to 325° F. Grease a 9 by 9-inch pan.

Beat together the sugar, Baked Vegan Margarine, baby food, corn starch, and vanilla until smooth and creamy. Stir in the flour and the nuts.

Spoon half the batter into the prepared pan; spread it out evenly. Cover the batter evenly with jam. Cover the jam with the remaining batter.

Bake for 50 minutes. Cool for about 10 minutes. Cut into 24 bars. One bar should do the trick.

INGREDIENTS

½ cup of a firmly packed brown sugar

½ cup of Baked Vegan Margarine

1 tablespoon of apricot baby food

½ teaspoon of corn starch

½ teaspoon of vanilla extract

1 cup of flour

½ cup of chopped walnuts

¼ cup of apricot jam

Gingerbread Cookies

Complex flavors with a fairy tale ending

Beat together the Baked Vegan Margarine and sugar in a large bowl. Add egg replacer, molasses, and vinegar and set aside.

In a separate bowl, sift together the remaining ingredients. Combine the dry ingredients with the margarine mixture and stir until it's all well mixed.

Refrigerate the dough for at least two hours or overnight. This will help the mixture become firm.

When you're ready to get baking preheat the oven to 375° F.

Form the cookie mixture into ½ inch balls and flatten, or roll them out onto a floured surface and cut into shapes using cookie cutters. Either method will do.

Place the cookies on cookie sheet and bake for 6 to 8 minutes until done. Cool the cookies thoroughly. Two cookies should get you baked.

INGREDIENTS

½ cup of Baked Vegan Margarine

½ cup of sugar

Egg replacer for 1 egg

½ cup of molasses

1 tablespoon of apple cider vinegar

2½ cups of flour

¼ teaspoon of salt

1 teaspoon of baking soda

1 teaspoons of ginger

1 teaspoon of cinnamon

½ teaspoon of cloves

½ teaspoon of nutmeg

Lemon Poppy Seed Cookies

So rich and moist, one batch is never enough

Preheat oven to 350° F.

Cream together the sugar, brown sugar, and Baked Vegan Margarine until smooth and creamy. To this mixture add the soy yogurt and vanilla and mix it all together thoroughly.

Add the remaining ingredients to the dough. Drop the dough by table-spoonfuls onto a cookie sheet and bake for 8 minutes, or until done.

Two cookies should get you baked.

¾ cup of sugar

¾ cup of brown sugar

½ cup of Baked Vegan Margarine

1 cup of soy yogurt

1½ teaspoons of vanilla

¾ teaspoon of baking soda

¾ teaspoon of salt

1 teaspoon of lemon zest

2½ cups of flour

¾ cup of poppy seeds

Coco Nutty Lime Cookies

You'll go nutty for the flavor of this Asian-inspired treat

Preheat oven to 375°F.

Cream the Baked Vegan Margarine, icing sugar, vanilla, coconut extract, lime juice, and lime zest in a large bowl until smooth. Gradually add in the cornstarch and flour, beating after each addition.

Stir in the ½ cup coconut, kneading if necessary. If the dough is crumbling, add a splash of lime juice or soy milk. Roll the dough into balls, about 2 tablespoons each. Set aside.

Pour the remaining coconut into a small bowl. Roll each cookie in the coconut, then lay on a parchment-lined cookie sheet. Sprinkle the rest of the coconut on top of the cookies.

Bake cookies for about 15 minutes or until firm and the bottoms are golden brown. Leave to cool on the cookie tray for at least 10 minutes before moving them to a cooling rack or they will crumble when you transfer them.

Make the lime glaze by combining all three ingredients together in a small bowl and stirring until smooth.

When the cookies are almost completely cooled, dip each one in the glaze and let sit until dry. Two cookies should do the trick.

INGREDIENTS

½ cup of Baked Vegan Margarine

¼ cup of icing sugar

¼ teaspoon of vanilla extract

¼ teaspoon of coconut extract

1 tablespoon of lime juice

¼ teaspoon of lime zest

½ cup of cornstarch

¾ cup of flour

½ cup of sweetened shredded coconut

⅔ cup of sweetened shredded coconut for rolling and sprinkling

LIME GLAZE:

2 tablespoons of lime juice

½ cup of icing sugar

¼ teaspoon of coconut extract

Fruity Loopy Shortbread
A taste of Christmas that will charm your inner fruit cake

Preheat the oven to 375° F.

Combine the flour, soda, spices, and cream of tartar together with a wire whisk.

In a large bowl, beat the Baked Vegan Margarine and sugar until fluffy. Add the baby food and cornstarch. Stir in the vanilla and (crumbled if you don't like bigger pieces) cup of candied fruit.

To the baby food mixture add the dry ingredients. Mix it all together well. The dough will be stiff. Roll the dough into 1-inch balls. Place the balls on an ungreased cookie sheet; flatten them ever so slightly.

Bake the cookies for 10 to 12 minutes or until lightly brown on the edges. Remove the cookies from the oven and then cover them with a glaze of icing sugar, soy milk/almond milk and vanilla while they're still warm if you want some extra sweetness.

Three cookies should get you baked.

INGREDIENTS

1 1/4 cup of flour

1/2 teaspoon of cream of tartar

3/4 cup of icing sugar

1 cup of candied fruit (like the kind you'd use in fruit cake)

1/2 teaspoon each of ginger, nutmeg, and cinnamon

1 teaspoon of vanilla

1/2 teaspoon of baking soda

1/2 cup of softened Baked Vegan Margarine

1 tablespoon of sweet potato baby food

1/2 teaspoon of corn starch

Index